WORLD WINDOWS
Maps

 HEINLE CENGAGE Learning™

 Young & Son Global, Inc.

When do you use a map?

Contents

Vocabulary

map

find

show

4

city

country

world

He wants to go to the park.
How can he find the park?

He can look at a map.

We look at a map to find places.

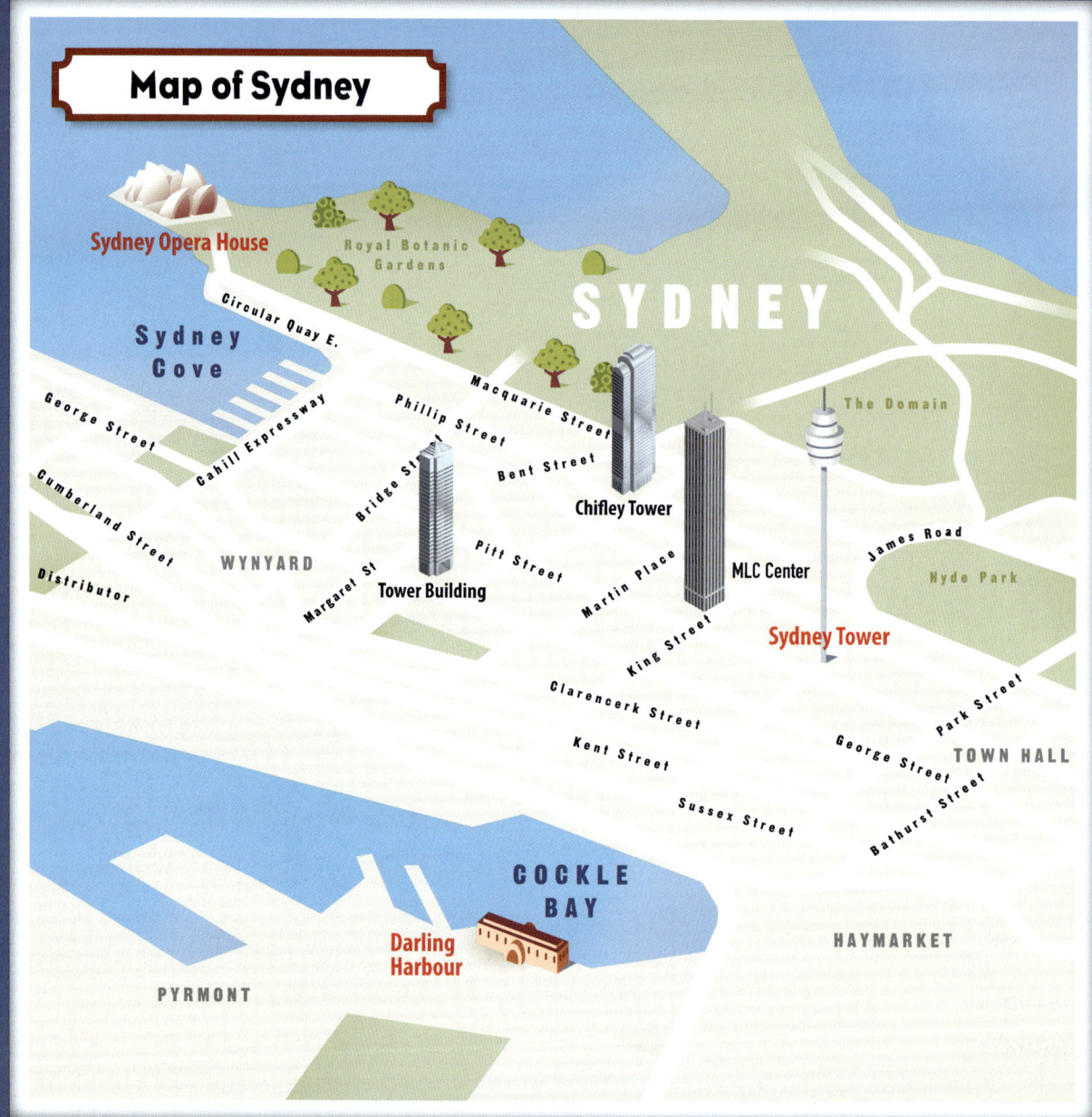

Map of Sydney

Sydney Opera House

Royal Botanic Gardens

Circular Quay E.

Sydney Cove

SYDNEY

The Domain

George Street

Cahill Expressway

Phillip Street

Macquarie Street

Chifley Tower

Cumberland Street

Bridge Street

Bent Street

MLC Center

James Road

Hyde Park

Distributor

WYNYARD

Margaret St

Pitt Street

Tower Building

Martin Place

King Street

Sydney Tower

Clarencerk Street

Kent Street

George Street

Park Street

TOWN HALL

COCKLE BAY

Sussex Street

Bathurst Street

Darling Harbour

HAYMARKET

PYRMONT

This is a map of a city.
It shows streets and buildings.
Can you find Sydney Tower
on the map?

Map of the United States

This is a map of a country.
It shows states and cities.
Can you find Los Angeles
on the map?

Map of the World

Greenland
DENMARK

ICELAND

NORWAY

EU[R]

UNITED
STATES

DENMARK

UNITED
KINGDOM

IRELAND

NETHERLANDS
BELGIUM

GERMAN

CANADA

FRANCE SWITZERLAND

ITA

NORTH
AMERICA

PORTUGAL SPAIN

TUNISIA

UNITED STATES

*ATLANTIC
OCEAN*

MOROCCO

ALGERIA

WESTERN
SAHARA

MEXICO

BAHAMAS

CUBA

DOMINICAN
REPUBLIC

MAURITANIA

MALI

NIGER

BELIZE

HAITI

JAMAICA

PUERTO RICO

SENEGAL
GAMBIA

BURKINA
FASO

GUATEMALA

HONDURAS

GUINEA-BISSAU

BENIN

NIGERIA

EL SALVADOR

NICARAGUA

GUINEA

SIERRA LEONE

CÔTE
D'IVOIRE

TOGO
GHANA

COSTA
RICA

PANAMA

LIBERIA

EQUITORIAL GUINEA

CAMERC

GABON

VENEZUELA

GUYANA
SURINAME
FRENCH GUIANA

COLOMBIA

*PACIFIC
OCEAN*

ECUADOR

SOUTH
AMERICA

PERU

BRAZIL

BOLIVIA

PARAGUAY

URUGUAY

CHILE

ARGENTINA

N

W   E

S

This is a map of the world.
It shows countries, continents,
and oceans.

RUSSIA

ASIA

PACIFIC OCEAN

KAZAKHSTAN

MONGOLIA

NORTH KOREA

SOUTH KOREA

JAPAN

GEORGIA
ARMENIA AZERBAIJAN
UZBEKISTAN
KYRGYZSTAN
TAJIKISTAN

TURKEY

CYPRUS
LEBANON
ISRAEL
SYRIA
JORDAN
IRAQ
KUWAIT
IRAN

TURKMENISTAN

AFGHANISTAN

CHINA

EGYPT

SAUDI ARABIA

UNITED ARAB EMIRATES
OMAN

PAKISTAN

NEPAL BHUTAN

INDIA

BANGLADESH

BURMA

CA

SUDAN

ERITREA YEMEN

LAOS

THAILAND

VIETNAM

CAMBODIA

PHILIPPINES

ETHIOPIA

SOMALIA

SRI LANKA

UGANDA
RWANDA
KENYA

MALAYSIA

TANZANIA

INDONESIA

PAPUA NEW GUINEA

INDIAN OCEAN

MBIA MALAWI

ZIMBABWE MOZAMBIQUE

MADAGASCAR

AUSTRALIA

AUSTRALIA

SWAZILAND
LESOTHO

NEW ZEALAND

ANTARCTICA

Can you find the Atlantic Ocean on the map?

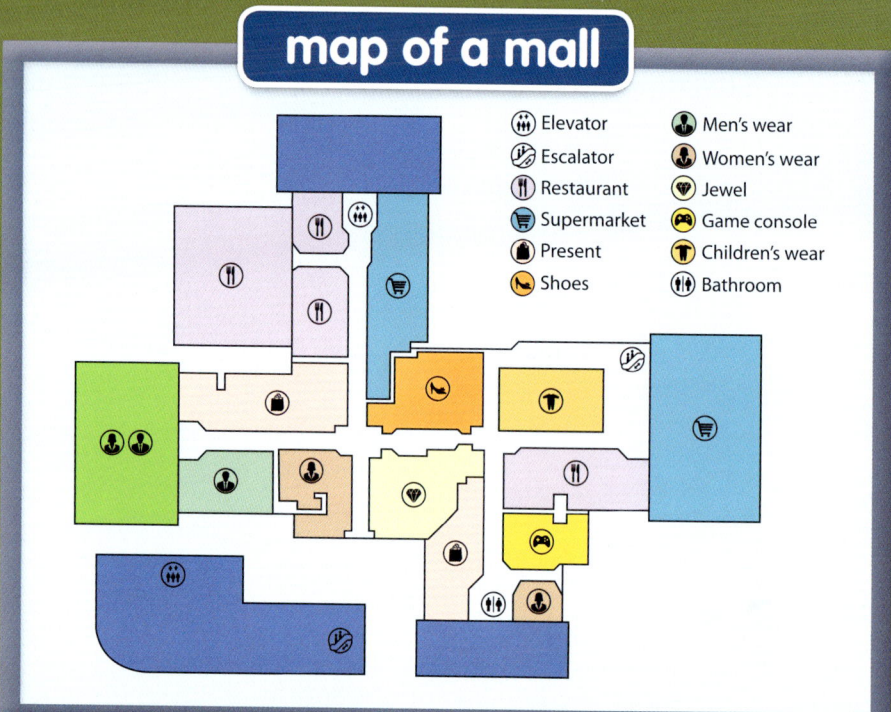

map of a mall

- Elevator
- Escalator
- Restaurant
- Supermarket
- Present
- Shoes
- Men's wear
- Women's wear
- Jewel
- Game console
- Children's wear
- Bathroom

treasure map

There are many other kinds of maps.
Different maps show different places.

map of a zoo

Axis Deer
Leopard
Humpback Whale
Eagle
Giraffe
Penguin
Wolf
Chimpanzee
Deer
Parrot
Seal
Hyena
Lion
ZOO OFFICE
Bear
wild dog
Monkey
Zebra
Tiger
Flamingo
Rabbit
Elephant
Owl
Buffalo
Rhinoceros

EXIT

ENTRANCE

PARKING

PARKING

ENTRANCE   EXIT   INFORMATION   EMERGENCY   RESTROOMS   RESTAURANT   FAST FOOD   PICNIC AREAS   FIREFIGHTING   TELEPHONE

What kinds of maps do you have?

What does each map show?

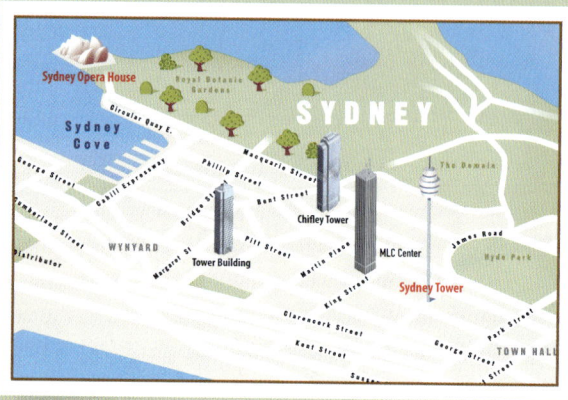

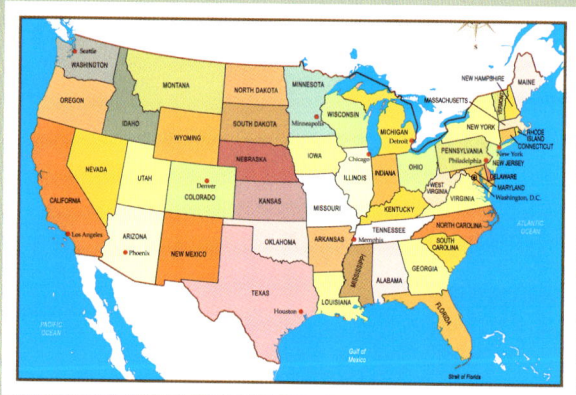

Use a Map

Map, map, use a map!
When you lose your way.
It will show you where to go.
You will find your way!

Map, map, use a map!
When you lose your way.
It will show you where to go.
You will find your way!

Index